REZ DOG

By Heather Brink

Illustrations by Jordan Rodgers

At night Rez Dog curled up to sleep in the woods near the gas station.

He wondered if he would ever find a family.

Rez Dog ate scraps of food he dug from the big trash can.

"Here you go, little Rez Dog," the store manager Mr. Thompson said handing the little scruffy pup a hot dog with lots of pickles.

"Eat this instead."

Rez Dog sat in the woods near the gas station watching the people and cars come and go.

There were noisy cars and smelly trucks. There were grumpy people. He saw loud teenagers and big families.

He'd lived with all of those types before.

Not this time!

There were also quiet cars with friendly people. One truck already had a puppy riding in the front seat with them.

And one car had a couple that looked like they were getting ready to go on a trip out of town.

He didn't see anyone who seemed just right.

Then he thought he saw someone who might be just right.

There was a small child peeking out the window of a pickup truck. She had brown hair and big brown eyes. She was with her mom.

"You remember what we've agreed to about a dog? It is your responsibility to walk, feed and clean up after, right, kiddo?" said her mom.

"Let's go ask the store manager, Mr. Thompson to see if he knows anything about this little rez dog."
?

"Sammy, that's just a rez dog, nobody owns him," said Mr. Thompson.
"But if you want to take him home, I'll give you some stuff."

On the way home, Rez Dog and Sammy were chewing on beef jerky. Sammy and Rez Dog were wearing garbage bags. Rez Dog was pretty dirty!

Mom tells Sammy when they get home,
"That rez dog is ***not*** *coming inside without a bath!"*
"Don't forget kiddo, Uncle's coming over."

Rez dog sat outside on the front stairs next to Sammy. He listened and waited with her.

"Hey there kiddo!
And hey there
little rez dog!"
It was Uncle.
"Hi ya Uncle!!!"
Rez dog got up to
sniff Uncle.
"I brought dinner
and some things
for your stinky
rez dog."

"Let's hose off that stinky rez dog and then we can give him a bath with the special flea shampoo I brought," said Uncle.

Then he carried the dog inside and straight to the bathtub.

Rez Dog did **NOT** like baths and he did not like being wet...

But now that he was clean he could explore the house!

That night Sammy was
way too excited, she couldn't sleep!

The next day, Sammy called her friend Mike. She showed him the dog.

They talked about names.

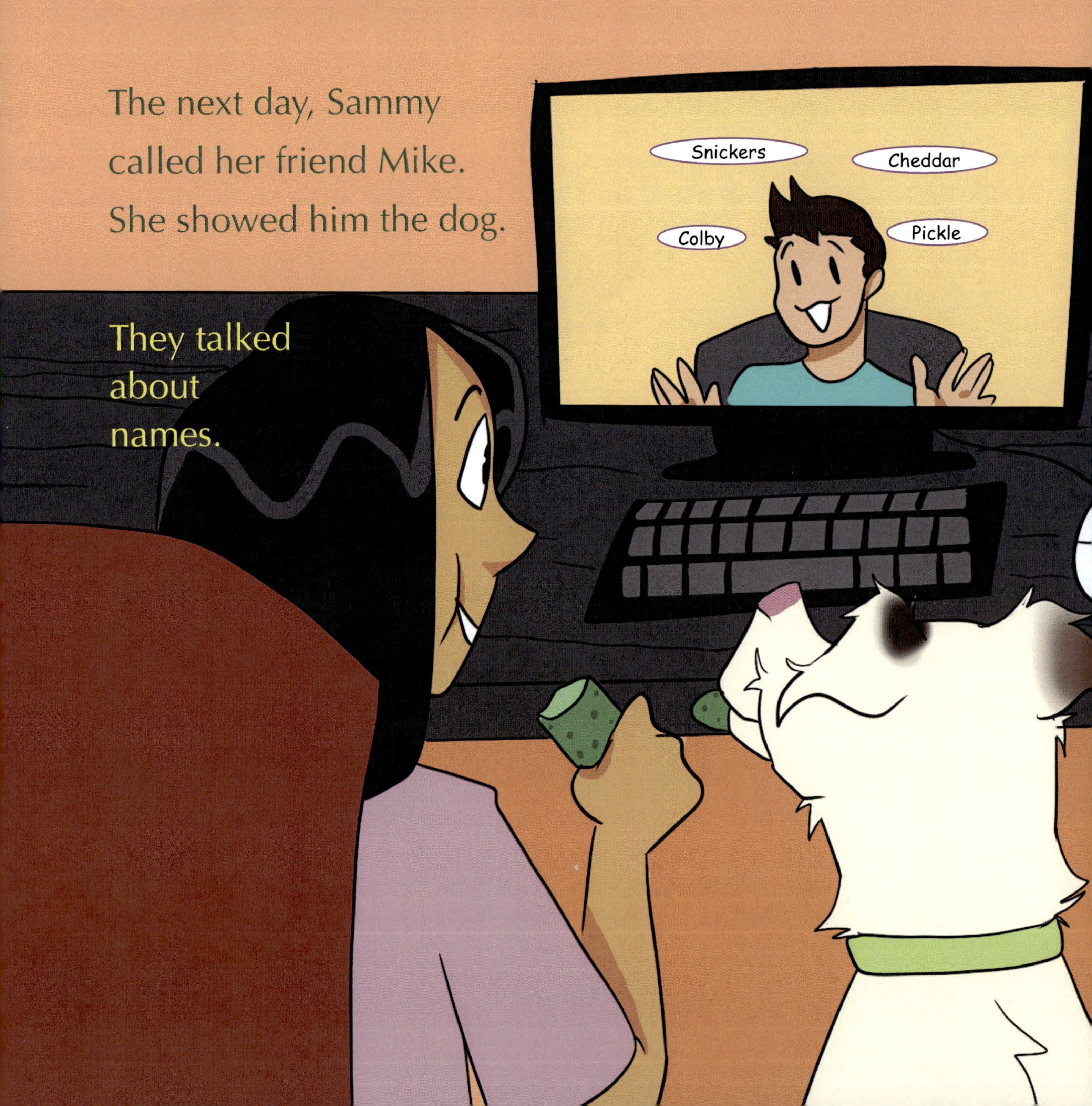

Later Sammy, Mom and Rez Dog go over to Uncle's house

"Uncle said you got a dog Sammy!

Let's see him,"

said Auntie.

"Let's feed this skinny pup
and all my grandkids too,"
says Grandma.

"So, do you have a name for this little Rez dog?"
asked Auntie.

"He needs to have a brave warrior name!"

"Pickle!"

"I see he picked out his own name!"

said Grandma.

"I guess so..."

"And he smells

like a pickle too."

Pickle was happy!
He had a home and a real name,
and a wonderful new family.

REZ DOG

By Heather Brink

Illustrations by Jordan Rodgers

ISBN 978-0-578-35933-5

Printed in the United States of America

Book cover and design by Marlene Wisuri
Dovetailed Press LLC
Duluth, Minnesota

Rez Dog
Books

Made in the USA
Las Vegas, NV
01 March 2023